Get Your Game Face On!

Kathy Toon

Good Sports Productions, Inc.
Berkeley, California

Good Sports Productions, Inc.

This publication is designed to provide accurate and authoritative information with
regard to the subject matter covered. Every attempt has been made to accurately
transcribe quotations used in this book. In the event of a question arising about
a quotation, we regret any error made and will be pleased to make the necessary
correction in future editions.

ISBN: 978-0-9824341-0-9

Published by
Good Sports Productions
1563 Solano Avenue, #124
Berkeley, CA 94707
Email: Kathy@coachtoon.com
Website: www.coachtoon.com

Book design by Brynn Breuner of Talewind Media
Cover design by Elisa Tanaka

Dedication

To Dr. Jim Loehr—
Thank you for always supporting me on this incredible journey.

Acknowledgements

First, the student would like to thank her teachers: Jan and Brian Parrott, Laurie Nelson, Gualberto Escudero, Sherri Stephens, Jan Brogan, Illana Berger, Rolland Todd and Jim Thompson.

I'd also like to thank my many students. To the athletes I coached at the University of San Diego, Mills College and University of California, Berkeley, thanks for helping me develop my art as a coach.

I am indebted to my colleagues for their contribution to my vision: the entire athletic department at Cal, the trainers and staff at Positive Coaching Alliance, Brynn Breuner, Elisa Tanaka, Jim Lobdell, Steve Seeley, Teri Cluck and John Bergez.

Finally, I'm grateful for the foundation in life—my family. Thanks to my parents, Bob and Joan; my sisters and brothers, Bonnie, Brian, Mary, Mike, Karen and Kevin. Big thanks to my sons Dylan and Alex for showing me a whole new world. The biggest thanks of all goes to my partner, Heather—my greatest teacher and my best friend.

Contents

Have you ever stopped to consider how elite athletes deal with the pressure of competition and consistently perform at their best? How do they summon and sustain their talent and skill when they need it, regardless of the circumstances? What does it take? What makes them so special? And how can you imitate their example?

Your goal as an athlete is to get your body to do what it's capable of doing under pressure. Each of us has our own unique peak performance "zone." This zone has a very specific chemistry behind it – one you can train for and learn to control. I call it your Game Face.

This book introduces you to the techniques that can enable you to have your Game Face on when you need it most—under pressure, when the stakes are highest. These techniques grew out of work pioneered by sports psychologist James Loehr that revolutionized the way tennis players train. Dr. Loehr's work transformed my athletes at the University of California, Berkeley, where I coached Division I women's tennis for fourteen years, from solid players into elite performers. The Game Face system is the result of the work head coach Jan Brogan and I did with hundreds of Cal tennis players. It is directly responsible for four NCAA doubles championships and one singles championships, not to mention numerous Pac-10 titles.

After many years of success with our own team, Coach Brogan and I started teaching our material to other athletes at Cal in a class entitled High Performance Training for Student Athletes. While teaching the course I began to wonder whether the system would work with other sports besides tennis. I spent five years working with Cal athletes and coaches applying the Game Face system to numerous sports. The results have been amazing. The Game Face System worked with every sport I encountered—from football, baseball, and volleyball to soccer, basketball, and golf—and more. For instance, I worked with one of our golfers on her Game Face Routine, and she went from the middle of the lineup to the program's top golfer and earned All Pac-10 honors. I also had success working with a couple of football players. Learning to solidify their Game Face Routines earned them positions in the starting lineup.

Now you can make the Game Face system your own. This book will tell you how. It will give you the principles and techniques you need. The hard work of applying them to your training—and your life—is up to you.

chapter one

Got Game Face?

Got Game Face?

Tiger Woods. Lisa Leslie. Tom Brady. They are among the world's greatest athletes. Time and again, you've watched superstars like these deliver the most amazing performances. Whether it's sinking the putt that wins the Master's, swishing the crucial free throw in the WNBA finals, or leading the drive that wins the Super Bowl, the greatest athletes play their best when the stakes are highest.

How do they do it? How do great athletes deal with the pressure of competition? How do they get their A game to show up in the heat of the moment? How do they regroup after making a mistake or losing their focus?

The Surprising Secret of Superior Performance

These questions intrigued sports psychologist James Loehr. Loehr sought answers by studying the performance of great tennis players. His research revealed a surprising secret: top tennis players used the time *between points* (plays) to "achieve the emotional balance and stable physiology needed for high performance" *(Loehr 1994, p. 90)*. More specifically, successful players followed a distinct pattern of activity between points, whereas poor competitors failed to complete one or more of these activities. Here is how Dr. Loehr put it:

> I spent years studying footage of top players—it was
> nearly impossible to determine a player's mental

toughness by simply observing how they perform during points. The between-point time reveals what is really happening in terms of mental toughness. From my studies over several years I discovered that the top mentally tough competitors consistently completed four rather distinct patterns of activity between points. Players with competitive problems however failed to complete one or more of these activities. From this understanding I developed a between-point training sequence of mental and physical activity modeled by the top tennis players *(Loehr 1988, p. 80)*.

The training system developed by Dr. Loehr dramatically changed training in tennis. And it turns out that the same basic emphasis on training for what happens "between points" works in other sports, too.

Think about it. Every sport at some point has down time between plays. In fact, many sports have more down time than actual playing time. Football, baseball, and volleyball, for example, are very similar to tennis in terms of between-play time. Golfers have even more time between shots. Swimmers, gymnasts, and track and field athletes have down time between events. By Dr. Loehr's principles, what athletes do between plays in all these sports is crucial to their performance. And that is just what I have found.

Consider Tom Brady, the quarterback of the New England Patriots during their undefeated regular season in 2007. Whether the game is safely in hand or the clock is ticking down and the game is on the line, Brady is known for his calming presence and leadership in the huddle, his ability to know the situation, make the right play, avoid turnovers, and keep the drive alive. If you observe him closely, you'll see that one key to his success is his consistency between plays. It's nearly impossible to tell whether the Patriots are winning or losing by looking at Brady after a play. He watches the outcome of each play with keen interest, but his reaction to what has just happened seems amazingly neutral. With his hands stuffed into his warmer he glances at the sidelines, acknowledges the call, and strides confidently to the huddle. In the huddle, Brady leans in and calmly calls the play. As he takes his position behind the center, he surveys the defense with poised intensity, points to the defensive scheme, and decisively calls out signals. Through all of this, Brady is the picture of focus and control.

> The definition of mental toughness is not letting anything get to you. It's just staying focused no matter what's swirling around you, just continuing to mentally fight through whatever obstacles there might be, whether that be a certain play or situation or a bunch of things that come up as a football player.
> –TOM BRADY

Or consider golfer Annika Sorenstam's playoff win at the 2006 U.S. Women's Open. Sorenstam was at her best, consistently hitting down the middle of the fairway and staying out of trouble. She missed only four greens in the playoff and put enormous pressure on her opponent, Pat Hurst. Here's what Annika had to say about her approach to the final day:

> I had to be patient. I went out there and relaxed between shots. I really didn't want to waste too much energy because it was such a long weekend, especially since the conditions were so tough. You think a lot. I think I'm more mentally tired than physically because you're trying to plan the shots. Some holes the elevation change, you're trying to plan the shot, what club,

how much is the wind, what kind of distance you have to add or subtract. It's just a lot of thinking and that wears me out.

To stay relaxed I talked a lot to my caddie, Terry. It was just a good way to relax and not really think about the game the whole time you're out there. *(LPGA.com 2006)*

Notice Annika's emphasis on the time between shots. Studying her performance, on this occasion and others, reveals a consistent pattern. It starts with her distinctive finish off her drive, where she's standing up straight and tall before she quickly pulls the club down to chest level as she watches her shot. After handing her club to her caddie, Annika walks purposefully toward her next shot. She often chats with her caddie and occasionally her opponent. As she nears her ball, all conversation ceases as she surveys the situation. If her opponent is to hit first, Annika

stands next to her bag with her hand grasping its rim and gazes toward the flag while watching the flight of her opponent's shot. When it's her turn, she grabs her club, stands a few feet behind the ball, and visualizes her shot. She takes one practice swing to get loose, and then walks to the ball, where she sets her feet, relaxes her arms, and looks at the target one last time. She takes just four or five seconds over the ball. By the time she swings, the foundation of her success has already been laid.

Examples like these reinforce what I found in my work with athletes at Cal. Most athletes today know that mental training is as important as physical preparation. The surprising secret of superior performance, however, is this: to maximize your performance on game day, you need to prepare physically and mentally for the *between-play* moments—those times when you're off the ball, going to the huddle, in the batter's box, or preparing to serve. Maximizing your between-play time will take you to an entirely different level of execution and competition.

I have found that this basic principle applies even to continuous-play sports such as soccer, lacrosse, and water polo. In these sports the clock continues to run and there isn't regular down time. However, as I examined these sports more closely, I discovered moments of sporadic down time that did have an impact on performance. I worked with athletes on how they spent their time during time outs, penalty situations, substitutions, intermissions between periods, and even during their "off-ball" time. Once again I found that in going for peak performance, every second counts and needs to be trained.

This powerful insight—known to few athletes today—is at the heart of the Game Face system. The system starts with what I call the Game Face Routine.

The Game Face Routine

Imagine you have an important competition tomorrow. How do you want to feel? Take a moment and brainstorm a list of feelings.

In my work with athletes, the following words often come up: *focused, confident, relaxed, joy, fun, calm,* and *energy* or *pumped.* What are they describing? It has many names: the "zone," "flow," "the ideal performance state," "treeing," "playing out of your head," and so on. I call it Game Face.

Many athletes experience high-stakes competition as threatening, anxiety-provoking, and even frightening. Yet top athletes typically respond with high focus, clarity, passion, confidence, excitement, and engagement. All great athletes get nervous—that's just part of the territory. The difference is great athletes learn to control their nerves. And when nerves do happen, they don't last very long. Instead, these athletes find the zone—they have their Game Face on.

In my terminology, getting into that zone is a product of faithfully following your Game Face Routine. This routine is an "on-the-playing-field" tool designed to help you deal with the pressures of competition. It consists of four steps that repeat during the course of competition. The specifics and sequencing of the steps will vary by sport; however, the steps themselves can be applied to any sport. I call them the 4 R's: Reaction, Recovery, Readiness, and Ritual.

Here's how one of my players, Amy Jensen, used this systematic approach, derived from Dr. Loehr's work, to win a record-setting three consecutive NCAA doubles titles.

Reaction

Amy's Reaction step started as soon as a point ended. No matter what had just happened, she trained herself to react in a very consistent manner. She had the first few seconds following the point to herself. It was key that she portrayed a strong, powerful, and confident image, no matter what! When she and her doubles partner won the point, Amy usually gave a small fist pump and did a small hop-step to turn around. If they lost the point (especially if she missed the shot), Amy faced a bigger challenge. She worked hard to eliminate anger from her repertoire. The use of deep breathing and disciplined posture in those first three seconds made all the difference in the world in dealing with anger. She also worked hard on controlling what came out of her mouth right after the point, moving from words of anger and disgust to words of challenge such as "Right back!" and "Come On!"

Recovery

The key to maintaining one's intensity for an entire competition is to balance the energy spent during the action with the energy recovered between plays. The purpose of the Recovery step was to allow Amy's body, mind, and emotions to recover from the point.

Amy would walk in the direction of her partner with her racket in her non-dominant hand and maintain a pace that allowed her to recover yet not lose her intensity. Once Amy met up with her partner, they would walk side by side to the area of the court behind the baseline. The intent was to recover energy and connect as a team at the same time. The conversation was minimal and always encouraging.

Readiness

The Readiness step occurred behind the baseline. This was the time when Amy would get mentally ready for the point. She and her partner would stand behind the baseline and discuss their strategy for the next point. They would discuss any pertinent information: What's the score? What are the weather conditions? What are the opponent's tendencies? Then they would decide what their objective was for the upcoming point: "Serve up the middle and look to poach," "Attack a second serve and come in," "Take the return up the line," and so on. They always maintained a strong and confident posture during their discussion.

Ritual

Amy's final step in maintaining her Game Face was physical preparation just prior to the next point. This is often referred to as Ritual. Rituals helped to deepen Amy's concentration and help her adjust her energy levels just prior to the action.

ritual

When it was her turn to serve, Amy's ritual started a bit behind the baseline. She wanted to approach the line with energy. After a quick check of her body— was she feeling flat or tight? Amy used her breathing to create the feeling of challenge. She set her left foot as close to the baseline as she could and bounced the ball three times with her weight just on her left leg. She then picked one technical piece of her serve to think about, such as "Keep my left side up" or "Quads be explosive." This technique kept her focused on the process of serving rather than the outcome. Finally, Amy would mentally see where she wanted to serve as well as feel and hear the contact she wanted to make.

When Amy's side was returning serve, her ritual was somewhat different. She would turn her back to the court and keep her eyes on the strings of her racket. Again she was doing a quick check-in with herself: was she tight, flat, loose, fired up? At this point she wanted to keep her focus internal and on her own game. When Amy was ready, she turned around to face the court and moved to the baseline with energy. She always kept her racket in her left hand while shaking out her right hand. Then she gently touched her right hand to her right leg to connect with her body. Mentally Amy focused on one technical cue that would help her hit the selected return, such as "Let the ball come in a bit" or "Stay low." She visualized and mentally felt the contact she wanted to make and her first step. Physically Amy crouched into a good athletic stance, her weight on her toes and her left foot forward. Just as the opponent's toss went up, she split step and was ready to move forward into her return.

Amy's Game Face Routine illustrates the essence of the 4 R's approach. As I said, faithfully following these four steps helped Amy win three national championships. You'll learn about each step in more detail in Chapter 2.

> Game Face allowed me to summon the emotions I needed during battle. It's the most powerful tool I've used.
>
> –AMY JENSEN, THREE-TIME NCAA CHAMPION (1998, 1999, 2000) (shown on page 11 and 12 playing with partner Amanda Augustus in 1998, and in the remainder of the chapter with Claire Curran, 2000)

The Game Face Training Program

How do Tom Brady, Annika Sorenstam, Amy Jensen, and other top athletes *consistently* demonstrate resilience, flexibility, and optimism even when faced with adversity? The answer isn't just that they have their own versions of the Game Face Routine. Consistent performers train each day so they can muster their Game Face when they need it most. What's more, they attend to the important details in life and create ways to maximize them so they have abundant energy available for performance.

What does this mean for you? It means building a training program that helps you to perform consistently at your highest level. The Game Face Routine will help any athlete achieve greater success in any single competition.

Without the proper training program, however, the 4 R's will just be "acting tricks" that work only on occasion. If you want to call upon your Game Face over the course of a tournament, a season, or a career, you need to train for it each and every day. The key is to create a customized Game Face Training Program, one that will support you in calling upon the 4 R's when you need them most.

> There are things in your life that you don't feel are quite right, so you change them....And you've got to tweak them every day because it is very easy to get out of balance and not have everything exactly as you would like to have it. It could be that you are sleeping too much or not sleeping enough. Or you're not eating enough or eating too much. You've just got to keep the right balance.
> −*TIGER WOODS*

Building your Game Face Training Program is not rocket science. It involves making simple lifestyle choices in four key categories: physiological, physical, mental, and daily life. As shown below, these choices are the basis of what I call the Game Face Performance Pyramid. They provide a foundation for the Game Face Routine you'll use during competitions.

What are those lifestyle choices? You'll learn about them in detail in Chapter 3. Here's a quick preview.

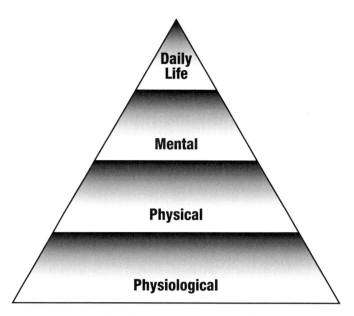

Figure 1. THE GAME FACE PERFORMANCE PYRAMID

PHYSIOLOGICAL

Your underlying physiology is the base of your Game Face Training Program. The dictionary defines *physiology* as "the functions and vital processes of living organisms." These vital processes include your nerves, muscles, circulation, breathing, and immune system. All are key to peak performance. Without a solid physiological base, you will not be able to drive the energy needed to train physically and mentally or attend to the requirements of your daily life. What you choose to eat and drink, along with your sleep habits, has a huge impact on these vital functions. For this reason, your Game Face Training Program must address these basic areas.

PHYSICAL

Top athletes know the connection between feeling confident and being physically fit. They also understand the role that peak practice plays in peak performance. The physical aspect of your Game Face Training Program encompasses the quantity and quality of your conditioning and practice sessions.

MENTAL

Baseball Hall of Famer Yogi Berra is credited with remarking that "ninety-nine percent of this game is half mental." Yogi's math may have been a little shaky, but his point was a good one—and it applies to every sport, not just baseball. Most athletes know that the mental aspect of performance is hugely important. It's common that the mental part of a sport is often what separates the "chokers" from the heroes. Yet, most athletes spend ninety-five percent of their time on physical training instead of devoting substantial time to a *mental* training program customized to the demands of their sport. Your Game Face Training Program won't make this mistake. It will prepare you to perform at your best mentally as well as physically.

DAILY LIFE

Physiology, check. Physical training, check. Mental training, check. What about the rest of your life? School? Family? Friends? Your car? Believe it or not, all these things have an impact on your performance. That means a solid training program needs to address the elements of your daily life. Your Game Face Training Program will.

Conclusion

At this point, you've got a bird's-eye view of the Game Face System. It has two main parts, the 4 R's that make up the Game Face Routine and the lifestyle choices represented by the Game Face Training Program. In the next two chapters, you'll take a closer look at each of the two parts of the Game Face system.

chapter two

The Game Face
Routine: The 4 Rs

The Game Face Routine: The 4 R's

You've already been introduced to the 4 R's that make up the Game Face Routine. I am convinced that this routine underlies all consistently great athletic performances. That doesn't mean you'll hear Eli Manning, Lorena Ochoa, or Tim Duncan talking about the 4 R's by name. They may never have heard of them in so many words. But if you look at the way these athletes actually perform, you'll find they are following the routine I'm about to describe.

reaction

Step one is Reaction. If you want to maintain your Game Face during competition, you must learn to control your reaction the instant the action stops. Your goal is to keep your Game Face even in the face of adversity. Yeah, I know—easier said than done!

To understand this critical step in keeping your Game Face on, you need to consider a little psychology. Take a look at Figure 2. This simple diagram underlies a lot of animal and human behavior. Let's take a dog, for example. Think of those TV commercials when a dog hears the sound of dry food being poured into the bowl and comes running to get its dinner. This is the classic "stimulus-response" phenomenon. The dog has learned that a certain sound is associated with the availability of food. So now, when the stimulus occurs (the sound of dog food being poured into the bowl), a response follows (the dog comes running).

Humans, too, learn to respond in certain ways to stimuli. But humans are slightly more evolved, and we experience a critical moment between stimulus and response. In this critical moment, we form our perception of what just happened, and the perception helps to determine our response. For example, we decide if the stimulus was "good" or "bad," and then we respond accordingly. In sports, this moment determines whether we take the High Road toward our Game Face or stumble down the Low Road to emotional upset and negativity. The High Road leads to superior performance. The Low Road leads to disappointment (see below).

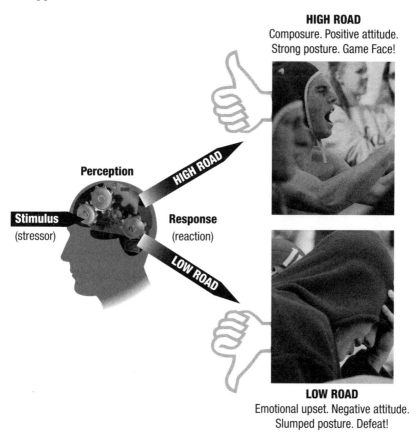

HIGH ROAD
Composure. Positive attitude.
Strong posture. Game Face!

LOW ROAD
Emotional upset. Negative attitude.
Slumped posture. Defeat!

FIGURE 2. THE STIMULUS-RESPONSE DIAGRAM

So what's a stimulus for an athlete? The key stimuli are what I like to call "stressors." They are things we have learned to respond to in ways that elevate our stress.

What stressors do you face in competition? Hostile crowds? Weather? Bad calls? Mistakes (yours or your teammates)? Aches and pains? Obnoxious competitors? Coaches? The list can go on and on. How do you respond in the face of these stressors? Do you keep your Game Face on, or do you display your negative emotions for all to see?

Too often we blame the stressors for our poor performance. But look at Figure 3 again. What side do you have control over? Clearly, you can't control the stimuli that come your way. The only thing you can control is your reaction to what happens. And because you *learned* the way you respond to a given stressor, you can *learn* to respond differently.

Top competitors learn to control their reaction so that they keep their Game Face on no matter what happens on the playing field. How do they do this? In general, there are two pathways to controlling your

reaction to stimuli or stressors. One pathway is your thoughts, and the other is what you do with your body. In other words, what do you say (either out loud or silently), and what do you look like between plays?

How we perceive something triggers our thoughts about it. The moment the action stops you have something to say about it. Your mind reacts long before your body does. In fact, the little voice inside your head directly impacts how your body responds. As soon as you are faced with a stimulus (or stressor), it is filtered through your values and beliefs. Your values and beliefs then determine your perception of the stimulus as a challenge or a problem.

Top competitors perceive stressors as challenges and believe that they can overcome them. Their little voice says, "Bring it on!" or "I can do this" or "This is tough, but I am tougher."

In contrast, poor performers see stressors as problems. They struggle with limiting beliefs about their abilities. Their little voice often says, "I can't" or "This is too hard" or "I'm not sure" or "This sucks."

Here's a really important point: Beliefs often become self-fulfilling. The good news is we can change our beliefs and thus our perceptions and ultimately our reactions to stressors. Our beliefs are just habitual thought patterns. Think the same thing over and over again, and it will eventually become an attitude or a belief. The trick to staying on the High Road in the face of stressors is to train "High Road" thought patterns. In a calm, non-stressful situation, consciously choose how you would like to think about the stressors you face in your life. Even better, write your thought down. Now repeat them to yourself over and over and over.

Training the way your body reacts is just as important. Dr. Loehr found that top tennis players learned to control their emotions by projecting a strong, fighting, and positive physical image as soon as a point was over. The next time you're watching top performers in action, watch what their bodies project between plays. Following a point, a top tennis player like Roger Federer will quickly turn around, place the racket in the non-dominant hand, and hold the racket head up as he walks energetically to take his position for the next point. In football, a top receiver like Marvin Harrison doesn't languish on the ground and look dejected after a tackle. Instead, he will bounce up as quickly as possible the moment the play is over and maintain a strong posture as he walks or jogs to the next huddle. In baseball, when an elite hitter like Derek Jeter swings and misses, he will keep his bat up instead of slamming it down in frustration and square his shoulders instead of slouching with dejection.

To be sure, personality type plays a role in our reaction styles. It's important to use a reaction style that fits your personality. Examples of athletes who display calm, neutral reactions include Federer, Steffi Graf, Annika Sorenstam, and NBA star Tim Duncan. Tiger Woods, LeBron James, and Serena Williams tend to be a bit more demonstrative. Allen Iverson, Lleyton Hewitt, and soccer star Abby Wambach can be downright fiery. Notice, though, that all these examples are on the positive end of the reaction continuum. Top athletes do not display dejection on the playing field. In other words, personality type is not an excuse to act out on the playing field in the name of "I gotta be me." Being at the whim of every emotion during competition is a sign of poor skill. It's the less successful athletes who wear their emotions on their sleeve. They show whatever they are feeling in the moment. If they are upset, they show it. If they are tired, they slump over and put their hands on their knees. If they are disappointed, they hang their heads and slump their shoulders. Unfortunately, the result is always the same: they fail to live up to their athletic potential.

Step one in your Game Face Routine, then, is about controlling your reaction as soon as the action stops. In all sports, the Reaction step involves doing these things:

1. Standing strong and confidently.
2. If a mistake has been made, using a mistake ritual to deal with it.
3. Saying or thinking something positive or challenging to yourself.

To get a feel for this step, let's try a little experiment. Stand up right now and show confidence with your entire body. Go ahead and try it. How do you display the feeling of confidence with every cell in your body?

I've done this with audiences hundreds of times, and the response is amazingly similar. When people stand up, their posture is impeccable—shoulders back, chin parallel to the ground, arms at their sides, legs strong—and their eyes are focused. If you did not stand up earlier, try it now. Take on this strong posture and see how it makes you feel.

Now try showing dejection. What is your body's posture now? If you're like most people, when you show dejection or discouragement, your shoulders slump, your head and arms hang down, your knees are bent, and your eyes are vacant. Again, try taking on this posture to see how it makes you feel.

I hope this exercise helps you to appreciate how training your body to react positively between plays can affect your emotions and, consequently, your performance. Of course, it's easy to respond positively when things are going well. Your true test is how you respond to mistakes, defeat and other negative events. Occasionally, top athletes will release some frustration or anger following a mistake. The difference is they do something that energizes them. They might aggressively slap their hands or a thigh but at the same time say or yell encouragement to themselves: "Come On!" "Right now!" "Let's Go!" They perform this ritual within seconds of committing the mistake, and then it's done and gone. The frustration doesn't linger into the next play.

recovery

Step 2 is Recovery. To maintain your Game Face Routine during competition, you'll need to take a moment to recover as much as possible of the physical, mental, and emotional energy you expend during play. Lack of a proper Recovery step often leads to quick, anxious movements and thoughts between plays. This can lead to problems with concentration, negative thinking, and nerves during competition.

Less successful athletes often rush between points or plays. In tennis, poor performers will walk hastily to retrieve the ball and plunge right into the next point. Rushing between points robs them of the peace of mind necessary to perform at a high level. In basketball, average players may remain "amped" after the whistle blows rather than slow down a bit to catch their breath. They walk, talk, and think at a quick pace as they move across the floor. Lower level volleyball players often move directly to their next rotation after a point. They fail to cherish the few seconds they have after coming together as a team following a point and setting up in the next rotation.

In contrast, top athletes use a variety of physical strategies to recover energy between plays, including the following:

+ deep breathing
+ keeping eyes focused on one thing
+ walking at a comfortable pace
+ stretching and shaking out their hands, arms, or legs

Between shots on the golf course, Lorena Ochoa walks at a consistent pace despite the score, breathes to relax, and keeps her eyes focused on the things immediately surrounding her. After the whistle blows signaling a foul, NBA star Steve Nash walks calmly and confidently toward the foul line with his eyes down and subtly shakes out his arms. Between points during a match, tennis star James Blake will walk over to the ball person, quickly wipe off with his towel, and occasionally grab a drink from his water bottle.

Actually refueling during competition is another way to recover energy. Top performers look for opportunities to grab quick bites of food or small drinks of water or sports drinks during pauses in the action as well as during intermissions.

readiness

The third step in your Game Face Routine is Readiness. The purpose of this step is to ensure that you are mentally prepared for the action to resume—that is, that you are aware of the situation and know your job during the upcoming action.

Readiness begins as soon as you *near* your re-start position. This step is often initiated by a signal that the action is about to start, such as a whistle, a time clock, or a gesture by a referee, opponent, or teammate. Upon detecting the signal, you pause momentarily, assume a strong posture, and reflect briefly on the following two questions:

1. What's the situation?

2. What's my job?

In other words, you quickly assess what's happening on the playing field, the time on the clock, the score, the weather conditions, and so on and then decide what your objective is for the upcoming action. You program your mental computer before you physically act.

So, for example, after the huddle breaks and prior to taking his stance on the line of scrimmage, Tom Brady will pause, survey the defense, and quickly review the play and his responsibilities. As the pitcher nears the mound, Mike Lowell, third baseman for the 2007 World

Champion Red Sox, will look around the field, take in the situation, and remind himself what he is responsible for on the upcoming play. Jenny Finch, Olympic Gold medal softball pitcher, pauses prior to taking the mound and assumes a strong, intimidating stance while she reviews the situation and her assignment.

To further illustrate the Readiness concept, Chart 1 summarizes the Readiness sequence for common situations in golf, football, basketball, and baseball or softball. Take a moment to visualize situations in your own favorite sport. See whether you can identify your re-start position, the signal to get ready, and the answers to the two key Readiness questions.

Re-start Position	Lie of the ball	Line of scrimmage	Side line of the free throw lane	Third base
Signal to get ready	Order of play and nearing lie	25-second clock	Referee hands ball to shooter	Pitcher stands behind mound
What's the situation?	350 yards to the hole, slight breeze	3rd and one, wet field	Opponent to shoot free throw	Runner on third
What's my job?	Lay up within 125 yards of hole	Secure the ball; follow blocks	Box out, go for rebound	Know outs; take correct infield position; hold runner

CHART 1. READINESS EXAMPLES

ritual

Ritual is the final step in your Game Face routine. Ritual is about physical preparation. The purpose of this step is to deepen your concentration and help you adjust your energy levels. Whereas Readiness begins when you *near* your re-start position, this step begins as soon as you *take* your final position just before the action resumes.

Visually, a ritual is the way you position yourself just prior to the action—how you set your feet and your hands, where you look, and the stance you take. Top athletes know that a ritual is a key step in ensuring consistent performance. For example, here's Tiger Woods talking about his pre-shot routine:

I have a pre-shot routine for every shot, but none is more important than when I have to hit a big drive in a pressure situation. Not only does my pre-shot routine allow me to focus on the task at hand, but it also keeps me in my natural rhythm. Every 300-yard bomb in my bag starts with a pre-shot routine that has a calming effect on me as much as anything.

My pre-shot routine, taught to me years ago by my father, didn't come naturally or easily. Like most kids I was of the grip-it-and-rip-it mentality. I had to learn patience and how to find my natural rhythm. Pop finally convinced me a pre-shot routine was necessary for consistency, and I've used the same one ever since.

Every shot begins behind the ball, and so does my pre-shot routine. I pick out a spot somewhere in the fairway where I want the ball to land and then move into the shot. I stand behind the ball holding the club while looking down my target line. I visualize my shot and pick an alignment spot a few feet in front of the ball. I take a forward step with my left foot, then step forward with my right foot. I then pivot off my right foot and rotating my body so it's square to the target line. I now move my right foot into position. Following a few minor adjustment and few waggles, then BAM.
(McDaniel 2002, p. 34)

Let's look at a few other examples of famous (or infamous) sport rituals:

Nomar Garciaparra in the batter's box: Nomar's ritual goes something like this. Scuffs a spot in the dirt with his back foot. Backs out of the box. Taps the toe of each cleat twice. Tap tap. Tap tap. Adjusts his helmet. Tugs his jersey a couple of times. Tap the cleats again. Tap tap. Tap tap. Re-checks the helmet. Obsessively adjusts, readjusts, and

re-readjusts his batting gloves. Takes a couple of practice swings. Finally steps into the batter's box ready for the pitch.

NFL quarterback Peyton Manning has a distinctive pre-snap ritual. He approaches the line, then races backward before reaching it; gestures with his left hand, gestures with his right; kicks his left leg; walks toward the line; places one hand over the other as if to put them under center; yells to the left, yells to the right; backpedals into the shotgun; kicks his left leg; and finally gets the ball and throws a pass.

Olympic gold-medal swimmer Natalie Coughlin at the blocks: During her shake-out routine she reaches both arms straight behind her back, palms out, until her hands touch. She hops up and down a few times on the pool deck to loosen up her body and then whips her bent arms over her head "like a motorist trying to flag down help," as Cynthia Gorney of the *New Yorker* described it. She performs these moves quickly and breaks into a brief smile and wave when her name is announced.

Then there's golfer Sergio Garcia's seemingly endless routine while he stands over every shot. Garcia sometimes waggles and re-grips more than thirty times per shot. His maddening ritual has drawn the ire of some of his fellow golfers. Many of them look away while Garcia waggles to distraction.

Chicago Bulls star Ben Gordon is among the NBA's most accurate from the line. As soon as the whistle blows, Ben heads to the free throw line. When he arrives, he takes a couple of deep breaths. He places the ball in his left hand and mimics his shot, including the follow-through, before taking the real one. Finally, he bounces the ball four times, bends his knees, and releases the ball.

What about you? Think about when you are performing well. What rituals do you use between plays? How do you ensure that your body is positioned for action? Do you bounce the ball two or three times before serving or shooting a free throw? Do you adjust your shirt sleeve, your cap, your helmet, or your gloves? Do you have a ritual for ensuring you adopt the correct stance? These seemingly "mindless" rituals are all about being physically prepared to execute the play. At this point, you should be thinking and visualizing only about the action right in front of you. There are no thoughts about technique or tactics. The goal is to perform instinctively and automatically, and rituals are designed to make it happen.

Getting your Game Face back on in competition

Creating your customized Game Face Routine is the first step in achieving a consistently high level of performance. The next step is to learn how to maintain your Game Face even when things happen that make you mad, frustrated, nervous, or discouraged. Let's look at some specific antidotes to several conditions that can cause you to lose your Game Face during competition.

anger

A big emotional hurdle is anger or negativity. Some athletes find that they don't get as nervous if they express their anger or negativity. Unfortunately, the chemistry of anger negatively affects their physiology. Coordination, balance, problem solving, and thinking ability may all suffer. Remember, "anger" is only one letter short of "danger"!

One of the quickest ways to handle anger in the moment is to use your breathing. Nothing controls and calms the emotions like full, deep breathing. This kind of breathing can help athletes let go of distractions, get re-centered, and refocus on the task at hand. If you feel angry, slow your breathing down and take a few long,

deep breaths. With proper breathing, you can actually increase your endurance, improve your reaction time, and stay calm, cool, and collected.

In addition to your breath, the things you say to yourself or out loud will either fuel or extinguish your anger. Thinking or saying positive things is incongruent with the emotion of anger. Since the body generally follows the mind, bombard yourself with positive language to over come the feeling of anger.

If anger is a consistent emotion for you on the playing field, you may need to do some off-field work as well. A huge step is to be aware of the issue and then admit it. Often we do not want to admit that our anger gets the best of us. Set a goal for yourself to deal with your anger issues and get support from your coaches and teammates to reach your goal. Chart 2 summarizes these antidotes to anger.

On Field	Off Field
Slow down	Notice it!
Take long, deep breaths	Admit it
Use positive language	Set a goal to deal with it

CHART 2. ANTIDOTES TO ANGER

Nerves are a normal part of competing. Even elite athletes get nervous. The difference is that they don't keep their attention on it. They acknowledge their "butterflies" and move on quickly. They don't allow negative self-talk into their minds.

When nerves go unchecked, however, they often lead to choking—the most feared state in athletics. When we choke, our muscles tighten, we can't think straight, things move too fast, and we feel out of control.

Unfortunately, many athletes hold their breath when they get nervous or uptight. If they do breathe, their breathing is usually shallow, which causes an increase in muscle tightness and blood pressure, making the situation worse. If your nerves get you too amped up, take long, slow, deep breaths.

Some athletes go the other way when they get nervous: their energy level gets too low. If this happens to you, quick, connected breathing can help to energize you. Here's how connected breathing works: Take a deep breath in through your nose, then exhale through your mouth. Before you finish your exhale, inhale again through your nose. Repeat two or three times. You will feel a burst of energy.

"A deer in headlights" is a fitting description for a person who's choking. Athletes who are choking often appear frozen, stuck, or moving in slow motion. To change this state, try bouncing around or moving your feet like a boxer. Jumping up and down on your toes increases blood flow and energy levels.

Choking can also lead to decreased blood flow to the hands and feet. Athletes experience this as tightness and may say they can't feel their hands, their stick, or the ball. If you experience this, try clapping,

slapping your thigh, or high-fiving with teammates. Techniques like this will help you get back into your body and to feel your hands and feet again.

On Field	Off Field
Breathe!	Admit it
Move, bounce around	Visualize working through it
Reconnect with your body	Use relaxation techniques

CHART 3. ANTIDOTES TO CHOKING

There are also things you can do off the playing field to help you deal with your nerves. First, admit that nerves are an issue. Then take deliberate steps to counter the problem. One very powerful technique is visualization, which we'll discuss in detail in Chapter 3. Relaxation techniques, such as meditation, yoga, Tai Chi, listening to music, and massage can also be very helpful. Chart 3 summarizes antidotes to choking.

Every athlete makes mistakes, even professionals.
It's not "making the mistake" that matters, it's how you respond to it.

Mistakes often produce anxiety in the moment. If this is true for you, review the on-field antidotes in Chart 3. Too often a mistake will literally stop us in our tracks. We stand still, hands on hips and shake our head. Unfortunately these behaviors just make the situation worse. Instead, *move*. Walk away from the mistake and bounce around or move your feet in some fashion.

Walk away from your mistake.

Another strategy to deal with mistakes in the moment is "Fake it 'til you make it." If your tendency is to feel dejected following a mistake, project "fake" confidence with strong posture and facial expression and shortly you will begin to feel it. In addition to assuming a strong, confident posture, call upon strong images, thoughts, and words that trigger confidence for you.

On Field	Off Field
Move! Increase your energy	Study role models
Fake it 'til you make it	Create a mistake ritual
Use strong images, thoughts, words	Visualize your new ritual
Use a mistake ritual	Video and review your mistakes

CHART 4. ANTIDOTES TO MISTAKES

A related antidote is to use a mistake ritual, a physical gesture (a clean one) that helps you bounce back quickly. Here are a few examples: tennis players often turn away from mistakes while placing their racket in their non-dominant hand; baseball or softball players may remove their hat (to let off steam) and wipe their brow to signal "no sweat"; basketball or soccer athletes may make a small "throw it way" gesture as they run back on defense. Off the field, create and visualize a mistake ritual that works for you, one that helps you bounce back quickly. Visualize and practice it. You can also study role models from your sport and try mimicking the way they handle mistakes. Finally, review video of yourself during stressful competition. Pay particular attention to how you deal with mistakes.

Crowd noise. Cameras. Tricks by the opponent. Fans. Family.

These are just a few of the distractions athletes face during competition. Maintaining focus and concentration for the entire contest is a huge task. Peak performance occurs when you are thinking in the here-and-now. Thinking about the past can be distracting, while thinking about the future can lead to choking.

Use the three-second rule to deal with distractions in the moment. Train yourself to deal with distraction in three seconds or less. Some athletes use trigger words to bring them right back to the action. Examples include "Right back," "Right here—right now," "Focus," and "Snap back." In addition, try a quick visualization where you see yourself effectively dealing with the distraction in the moment.

An off-field process for dealing with distractions involves listing all the possible things that might distract you. Once you have your list, then brainstorm ways to deal with each one. If you get stuck,

seek input from your coaches or more experienced teammates. Then visualize your new rituals. Chart 5 summarizes antidotes to distractions.

On Field	Off Field
Use the three-second rule	List all possible distractions
Use trigger words	Brainstorm responses
Visualize your responses	Visualize your new rituals

CHART 5. ANTIDOTES TO DISTRACTIONS

Conclusion

In this chapter, you learned in detail about the 4 R's that make up the Game Face Routine: Reaction, Readiness, Recovery, and Ritual. Using this routine between plays can enhance your performance in any sport. To maintain your Game Face even when adversity strikes, develop and practice antidotes to common situations such as anger, nerves, mistakes, and distractions.

Top athletes have learned to control their Game Face and access it at will. You, too, can do this, but like any developed skill, it demands training. We will cover this in depth in the next chapter as we consider the Game Face Training Program—the foundation of your performance pyramid.

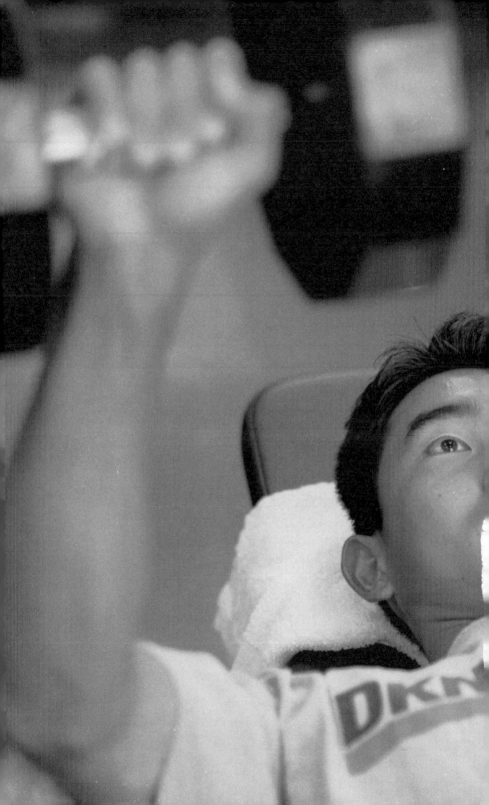

chapter three

The Game Face Training Program: 14 Key Performance Areas

The Game Face Training Program: 14 Key Performance Areas

Many athletes assume that Game Face is a state reserved for the Tiger Woods' of the world, but as you know by now, I don't believe this is the case. Most athletes can recall at least one performance in which they could seemingly do no wrong. Their execution was flawless, and they performed without really thinking about what they were doing. They had their Game Face on.

Is it possible for *you* to learn to call upon your Game Face in the heat of competition—consistently? Yes! Game Face is what psychologists call a learned response. That means it comes from experience, not instincts or genes or anything else you are born with. And in the context of sports, experience means one thing: training.

FIGURE 3. THE GAME FACE PERFORMANCE TRIANGLE

Your Game Face has a very specific chemistry behind it. We perform differently under pressure because the stress of competition actually causes our chemistry to change. The key to being a consistently strong competitor lies in learning to control your chemistry. Some athletes learn to control their chemistry through trial and error, while others never learn to. Based on Dr. Jim Loehr's work in tennis, we now *know* that athletes can train to control their chemistry and thus their Game Face.

Believe it or not, Game Face is not all mental. It is a multidimensional state, a unique set of interactions between physical, mental, and emotional factors, as shown in Figure 3.

The emotional side of this triangle represents your *feelings.* In competition, athletes with their Game Face on are driving feelings of confidence, energy, optimism, and calm. The mental side of the triangle represents your *thoughts* and *images.* Game Face thoughts and images center on executing the important tasks at hand. Lastly, the physical side of the triangle represents what you do with your *body,* or what you look like on the playing field.

The emotional, mental, and physical components of performance are inseparable.

They speak to one another through the language of biochemistry. The link between the mind and the body is the limbic system, a set of brain structures located at the core of the brain. The limbic system acts as a switchboard connecting the brain to the network of nerves throughout your body. The limbic system sends messages from the brain to the body's organs. Once these messages reach their destination, they stimulate the release of chemicals directly into your bloodstream. In other words, your Game Face has a specific chemical composition. When you are wearing your Game Face, you are sending very specific messages through your limbic system, resulting in what Dr. Loehr calls the Ideal Performance State.

All this means that what goes on in your mind has a direct effect on your body and vice versa. Your thoughts prompt certain emotions that in turn have bodily or physiological consequences. For example, thoughts about losing can lead to feelings of fear and anxiety. Those feelings cause various physiological responses: increased heart rate, shortness of breath, muscle tightness, narrow vision, and reduced blood

physiological

1. Nutrition
2. Hydration
3. Sleep

physical

4. Conditioning
5. Practice
6. Rehearsal

mental

7. Self-Talk
8. Focus
9. Visualization

daily life

10. Time Management
11. Academics
12. Fun

13. Relationships
14. Environment

CHART 6. 14 KEY PERFORMANCE AREAS

flow to the hands and feet. Those bodily sensations, in turn, can cause even more fear and anxiety. All of these responses stand in the way of your performing at your best. The same is true on the positive side: positive thoughts lead to feelings of energy, fun, and challenge. These feelings in turn produce positive physiological responses, which lead to even more positive thoughts and feelings.

I indicated in Chapter 1 that this training consists of learning to make sound choices in four broad categories: physiological, physical, mental, and daily life. Within these four categories, there are fourteen key performance areas that form the foundation of your Game Face, as shown in Chart 6. In this chapter, you'll be introduced to each of these critical areas.

Now here's the key point: this virtuous cycle can be trained. The 4 R's of the Game Face Routine will help you drive your Game Face during a competition. But the state of your Game Face, as well as your ability to access it, depends on a combination of physical, mental, and emotional training. If you want your Game Face to show up consistently over the course of a tournament or a season, you must train for it on a daily basis.

Physiological

Imagine trying to communicate without being allowed to use any vowels in your words. Imagine how limited your vocabulary would be and how you would struggle to get your point across. The same is true when athletes neglect or underestimate the value of their physiology.

Physiology is the foundation, the structural base for supporting the entire Game Face system. Unfortunately, athletes often do not appreciate how important their daily choices are in this area. Many will work hard to condition themselves

physiological

but neglect the importance of sleep, nutrition, and hydration. In college sports, even at the Division I level, most athletes are sleep-deprived, undernourished, and under-hydrated. As a result, they compete with a limited physiological vocabulary and have access to only a portion of what they're capable of achieving. When you pay attention to physiology, you maximize your potential as an athlete.

NUTRITION area #1

Nutrition is a key component of high-performance training. The foods you choose to eat will fuel your body, giving you the nutrients and energy you need to achieve your goals. As an athlete you need to consume enough nutrients to build strong bones and muscles; enough vitamins and minerals to keep your cells and organs functioning properly; and enough calories to provide sufficient energy for training and competition. By the same token, sporadic eating habits deprive your body of the fuel it needs, forcing your physiological system to try to compensate. When you skip breakfast, for example, your body is forced to draw on energy reserves stored in the liver. When this supply runs low, your blood sugar levels go down, and you become tired, cranky, hungry, and unable to focus. Research shows that skipping breakfast diminishes memory, performance on proficiency tests, and reaction time, whereas consuming a light meal in the morning enhances alertness and productivity.

Your body needs forty different nutrients to maintain good health. Essential nutrients include carbohydrates, proteins, fats, vitamins, minerals, and water. Trying to consume over forty nutrients is a lot to manage on a daily basis. In an effort to simplify this process, the U.S. Department of Agriculture developed the famous Food Guide Pyramid (see Figure 4). Although there are many opinions about the pyramid, it can be quite helpful when used as a basic scheme for guiding our food choices. It is not meant to be taken literally and needs to be adapted

Daily Food Intake

Fats, Oils, Sweets:
Sparingly

**Dairy–milk,
yoghurt, cheese:**
2–3 servings

**Protein–meat, fish,
eggs, beans, tofu:**
2–3 servings

Veggies:
3–4 servings

Fruit:
3–4 servings

**Bread, cereal,
grains, pasta:**
6–11 servings

FIGURE 4. THE FOOD GUIDE PYRAMID

to individual situations. (The Department of Agriculture now allows people to customize the pyramid and create individualized eating plans at www.mypyramid.gov).

The Food Guide Pyramid groups sources of needed nutrients into five major food categories. At the base of the pyramid are the foods that should be consumed most often, with recommended servings per day decreasing as you go up the pyramid. At the tip of the pyramid is the category Fats, Oils, and Sweets. These foods and food ingredients should be consumed sparingly to avoid excess calories and fat.

The basic message of the pyramid is simple: eat a variety of nutritious foods.

Here are some more specific pointers to keep in mind: Eat plenty of grain-based foods. These foods are rich in carbohydrates, which provide your body with the energy it needs throughout the day. Some examples include pasta, rice, bread, and cereal. Go for at least six ounces of grains each day, making sure at least half of them are whole grain. (Look for the phrase "whole grain" on the ingredient list.) Note: one slice of bread or a one-half cup of pasta equals one ounce.

training tip ▶ Eat a variety of healthy foods.

When it comes to vegetables, be creative and colorful. Shoot for two and a half cups per day. Salads make this task easy. Start with greens and add carrots, tomatoes, spinach, peppers, and other seasonal vegetables. Work in one to two cups of fruit or juice each day. Smoothies are a great way to meet your goal.

Get calcium from dairy products. Calcium is essential for strong bones. Your target here is three cups of low-fat milk or yogurt per day.

Consume sufficient protein. Protein is necessary for building strong muscles. Classic sources include meat, poultry, fish, dry beans, eggs, and nuts. Aim for five ounces daily. One serving of meat is roughly equivalent to the size of your fist, or one egg, or one-half ounce of nuts.

Cut down on caffeine. While caffeine increases alertness and arousal, it is associated with edginess, and its effect in high-stress situations is unpredictable. Reduce your caffeine consumption by switching to decaf coffee or tea, replacing caffeinated sodas with fruit juice, and replacing chocolate with some other comfort food.

Snack strategically. The content, timing, and frequency of your snacks are extremely important. Strategically snacking throughout the day stabilizes mood and energy levels and raises your metabolic rate. The performance benefits include better concentration, positive energy, and improved emotional control. Nutritious snacks include fresh fruit, bagels, low-fat yogurt, pretzels, Fig Newtons, PowerBars, low-fat soup, vegetables such as carrot and celery sticks, and popcorn.

Indulge yourself—occasionally. It's ok to treat yourself to sweets once in a while. Remember, moderation is the key.

HYDRATION performance area #2

You've heard of dehydration, the excessive loss of water in the body, and you probably know it can be dangerous and even life-threatening. The opposite state is *hydration,* or having sufficient water in your body.

Why is hydration so important? 70 to 80 percent of the human body is made up of water. Water is the most important nutrient for athletes. It is an athlete's cooling system, it gets rid of the by-products from training and it is essential for energy production. It is normal for an athlete to lose between two and five pounds of water during hard practices and competitions. Just two pounds of water loss can decrease your reaction time, coordination, speed, mental acuity, and perception.

Drink at least six to eight glasses of water each day. It's a key recovery strategy!  training tip

~~perf~~**SLEEP**~~ormance area~~ **#3**

Along with food and water, sleep is one of the most important recovery tools for an athlete. Lack of sleep makes us irritable; impairs our motor skills and our ability to think, to both make decisions and be creative. We are more likely to get upset and act out.

Unfortunately, we are a sleep-deprived country—and proud of it. According to James Maas, professor of psychology at Cornell University and author of *Power Sleep*, an estimated one third of the population suffer from sleep disorders. Many Americans have the notion that surviving on little sleep is macho. According to Maas, Americans have "habituated themselves to low levels of alertness. It's pathological behavior that's becoming a national epidemic." *(Maas, 1998, p. 20)*

training tip ▶ To improve your quality of sleep, try the following:

1. Get up and go to bed within a half-hour of the same time—preferably early.

2. Develop sleep rituals and follow them every night. For example, use something to help you relax and fall asleep. You might try reading a book, watching television, practicing visualization, meditating, practicing yoga, or taking a bath.

How Much Sleep Do You Need?

Humans are creatures of habit. To get the maximum benefit from sleep, we need to establish consistent patterns of getting up and going to bed to protect our sleep cycle. The precise amount of sleep one needs is highly individual and depends on a number of factors, including age, amount of physical activity, and levels of stress. Although the typical adult sleeps seven and a half hours a night, that's only an average. Some people need more sleep, while others need less. Also, virtually everyone's needs change with age. For instance, infants and children can require as much as sixteen to twenty hours of sleep per day, teenagers up to ten hours, and older people far less. Whatever your particular needs are, the bottom line is that you should wake up feeling relatively refreshed, and you should generally not feel exhausted during the day.

Naps

Most people experience the urge to rest in the early or mid afternoon between roughly 2:00 p.m. and 4:00 p.m. An afternoon nap of as little as five minutes can provide substantial physiological and psychological recovery. Afternoon naps can also increase energy, concentration, alertness, and motivation.

Find a quiet spot and lie down for five minutes between classes or before practice. This may help you feel awake and refreshed for your next activity.

Physical

Most athletes understand the physical aspect of training best. Game Face athletes take physical training to another level. They understand that every practice, every repetition, and every exertion is preparation for game-time competition and that every rep, sprint, dribble, throw, stroke or swing counts. Imagine if you always practiced with more intensity than you feel during competition. This caliber of training would condition you to compete at a peak performance level, and would make your game-time decision making and execution second nature.

CONDITIONING performance area #4

Conditioning is about more than bodily strength, flexibility, and endurance. There is a direct relationship between levels of physical fitness and mental and emotional performance as well. Physical training helps adjust the chemical balance in the nervous system. Exercise functions as a stimulant, causing an increased production of endorphins —neurotransmitters produced in the brain that reduce pain, enhance pleasure, and help you relax. The fitter you are, the more physical, mental, and emotional stress you can handle, and the higher your confidence will be.

> **Stress is the stimulus for growth and recovery is when you grow.**
> *–DR. JAMES LOEHR*

Working hard, though, is only half the equation. The best athletes balance their hard work with quality R & R (rest and recovery). All too often coaches and athletes focus just on the work side of the equation and forget about the vital R & R side. One without the other is a formula for disaster.

A popular belief in our culture is if a little is good, more must be better. However, work without rest leads to overtraining, burnout, and injury—where you are forced to rest because your body breaks down.

training tip ▶ Balance periods of intense training with periods of rest and recovery.

Proper training balances equal parts work with equal parts rest. Following a single training session with a period of rest and recovery and each training phase (weeks or months) with a recovery phase (days or weeks) actually enables an athlete to withstand higher and higher levels of intensity (see below).

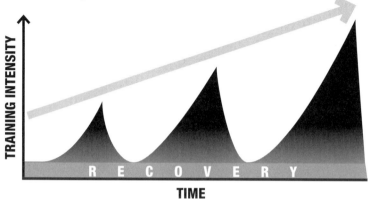

FIGURE 5. TRAINING PHASES FOLLOWED BY REST AND RECOVERY

PRACTICE performance area #5

Nothing can replace the endless hours of practice that are required to make physical skills automatic. If you want to enter the zone consistently, you must go onto the playing field physically prepared. Your strategy must be in place, and your technique must be trained so it is automatic.

Consistent high-level performance comes from consistent high-level practice. Top athletes practice the way they want to perform. They often make practice harder than competition, so when the time comes to perform they are ready. Here are some specific pointers to assist you in having peak practices. Most of them also apply to getting ready for a competition.

> "If you practice the way you play, there shouldn't be any difference. That's why I practiced so hard. I wanted to be prepared for the game. I practiced hard enough that the games were often easier. No one can turn it on without preparing themselves in practice. I took pride in the way I practiced."
> –*MICHAEL JORDAN*

Develop a Pre-Practice Preparation Plan

It is very important to make a successful physical, mental, and emotional transition from "student" or "worker" or "parent" to "athlete" prior to a practice. That's why you need to develop a pre-practice prep routine, one that will help prepare you for peak practice.

Physical transition: What do you need to do to be *physically* ready for practice? Possible suggestions: eating a light snack; drinking water or a sports drink; getting treatment at the training room; practicing a routine for changing into your workout clothes or uniform.

Mental transition: What do you need to do to be *mentally* prepared for practice? Possible suggestions: reviewing your training notes;

selecting one or two objectives for practice and writing them down (for example, "to give my best effort for the entire time," "to nail my landing on the vault" or "to work on my free throw percentage").

Emotional transition: What do you need to do to create the *feelings* you need for peak practice? Possibilities include listening to music on the way to practice, to either relax or to pump up; creating five minutes of quiet time to visualize having a peak practice; talking and laughing with someone; smiling!

Have a Contingency Plan Ready

We all have those days when we "wake up on the wrong side of the bed" and find ourselves feeling physically or emotionally out of sorts. We may be angry, cranky, sad, too "amped," or too tired. These feelings can get in the way of a good practice and often affect our teammates and coaches as well. You can deal more effectively with these "off" days if you develop a contingency plan for them. Here are some possible elements of an effective plan:

+ positive mental imagery
+ upbeat music
+ humor (with teammates, via comedy tapes, YouTube clips)
+ positive self-talk
+ wearing a big smile

Know What Distracts You and How to Deal with It

What distracts you during practice or competitions? Someone in the stands you care about or want to impress? Family or relationship problems? The media? Teammate issues? Your coach? High expectations? The prospect of playing a big rival? A new competition site? Remember that what you focus on grows. If you keep focusing on the distraction, it will only get bigger in your mind. The trick is to give your mind something else—something constructive—to focus on, such as feeling each muscle while you stretch; watching the ball so closely that you see it rotate; and exhaling every time you hit, throw, shoot, or kick the ball.

training tip ▶ Great preparation leads to great practice.
Great practice leads to great performance.

Be Prepared to Raise or Lower Your Energy

There are times when you will need to raise your energy level prior to practice or competition. If you need to psyche yourself up, try one or more of the following:

+ warming up faster or harder
+ using dynamic imagery
+ listening to upbeat music
+ finding a place where you can yell or scream
+ moving around

And then there are times you will need to calm down just prior to practice or competition. If this is the case, try the following:

+ listening to mellow music or a relaxation tape
+ doing progressive muscle relaxation
+ taking long, deep breaths
+ using calming imagery
+ meditating
+ stretching
+ sitting quietly with your eyes closed

Practice your techniques for raising or lowering energy so they will be ready for game day.

REHERSAL #6

If you want your Game Face to show up reliably in the heat of battle, you need to practice it every day. That means rehearsing the 4 R's diligently so that they become second nature.

In the beginning, using the Reaction, Recovery, Readiness, and Ritual steps during every break in play will probably seem forced and awkward. This is a natural part of learning any new skill. If you've ever tried to learn to play the guitar, you know that stretching your fingers into chords feels awkward and painful at first. Yet with practice, the movements become automatic. The same is true in sport. Stretching yourself into new territory is uncomfortable but will eventually become automatic with practice.

The key is to rehearse putting your Game Face on every day, even when you're not competing. Visualize yourself in competition. What would you see, hear, and feel? Put yourself in a strong, confident body posture. Feel yourself putting your Game Face on. In addition, study professional athletes you respect and admire. What are they doing between plays? How do they hold themselves? Practice imitating their tactics: their posture, their facial expression, and their rituals. Do a dry run of your Game Face Routine. Walk through your routine on the playing field without an opponent. Work the bugs out before you use it under pressure. And then, bring it to competition. Have someone record you on video so you can study your behavior and demeanor between plays. Do you keep your Game Face on? How do you do when things are going well? When they aren't going well? What stressors cause you to lose your Game Face?

training tip ▶ Rehearse the 4 R's until they become second nature.

Practice. Practice. Practice. Rehearsing your Game Face Routine during workout sessions, practices, and even as you go about your everyday life will help you access your Game Face when you need it most—in the heated moments of competition.

Mental

Game Face athletes know that training the mind is every bit as important as training the body. As Mia Hamm has said, "The most important attribute a player must have is mental toughness" *(Mack and Casstevens 2001, p. 24).* Mia makes clear that all performance is not purely physical, because what happens between your ears is critical to what happens during a game. Before you can win, you must have the will to prepare to win. That's why conditioning your mind is just as vital a part of the Game Face Training Program as conditioning your body.

SELF TALK performance area #7

Self-talk are the phrases we hear inside our heads. It's important to control that little voice in your head (the one that just said, "What little voice?"). Unfortunately for most of us, the little voice is often negative and critical. Common examples of negative self-talk include:

+ "I'll never be able to do that."
+ "I'm not smart enough."
+ "I'll look like a fool."
+ "I've never succeeded at that before— why should this time be different?"

We build strong, supportive self-talk in the same we build physical strength—through repetition. Just as consistently lifting weights builds physical strength, consistently "up-lifting" your thoughts builds mental strength. Unlike physical exercise, you cannot over-train your supportive self-talk muscle and you never wake up sore the next day!

Practice talking to yourself the way good coaches or teachers would. They are tough on you about things you can control, and they never give up on you.  **◄ training tip**

Focusing on the good may be natural for you if you were raised to be a positive thinker. But many of us have the habit of thinking negative and pessimistic thoughts. Years of repetition strengthen this habit. The key is to identify when and where your self-talk breaks down and to intervene with affirmations that foster strength, grace, and consistency in performance. Affirmations are self-talk statements that express positive attitudes or thoughts about oneself. The most effective affirmations are believable and vivid. A famous example comes from Muhammad Ali: "I am the greatest! I float like a butterfly and sting like a bee!"

The 5 Watches
Watch your thoughts,
They become your words.
Watch your words,
They become your actions.
Watch your actions,
They become your habits.
Watch your habits,
They become your character.
Watch your character,
It becomes your destiny.
–ATTRIBUTED TO FRANK OUTLAW

FOCUS**ormance area #8**

Peak performance on and off the playing field occurs when you are focused on the important things in the here and now. Focus is about effectively dealing with distracting stimuli and keeping your attention on what's important right now.

Athletes are bombarded with all kinds of sights and sounds during practice and competition. There are also internal distractions, such as thinking about the past or the future instead of the task at hand. These distractions can lead to choking. (In a *Peanuts* cartoon, Lucy explains how she muffed a fly ball by saying, "The past got in my eyes.") Staying on the high road and maintaining your Game Face under pressure requires you to screen out the bombardment of stimuli coming at you and key in on the important things.

How do you decide what's important? A good place to start is to separate the things you can control from the ones you can't. For example, look at the list in Figure 6. What items are in your "circle of control"? What items fall outside the circle?

- Playing time
- Attitude
- Work Ethic
- Teammates
- Thoughts
- Coaches
- Motivation
- Effort
- Teachers
- Scholarship
- Learning
- Winning

NO CONTROL

ZONE OF CONTROL

FIGURE 6. CIRCLE OF CONTROL

When you stop and think about it, we really have control only over ourselves. We can't control the people or things outside of us. We have no control over what other people think of us, what they say about us, or what they do (offer us a scholarship or give us playing time). We have no control over winning or losing, the weather, or the behavior of fans, opponents, teammates, judges, or referees. Champions keep their focus on the things they directly control: their attitude, work ethic, thoughts, motivation, effort, and learning. In addition, champions focus on the process, not the outcome (winning, scholarship offers, playing time). They keep their attention on the things in their circle of control that will put them in the best position to succeed.

Learning to meditate, taking yoga, and practicing breathing exercises can help you minimize distractions and stay focused on the here and now. ◀ **training tip**

It's also important to focus on what you want to happen rather than what you do not want to happen. Remember, "You can't do a don't do." How often do you say to yourself, "Don't miss," "Don't strike out," "Don't fumble," or "Don't turn the ball over"? Good luck. It's like someone asking you not to think of a pink elephant. (What image just popped into your mind?) When you focus on what you don't want to do, your mind and your body don't hear the word "don't." They hear "miss," "strike out," "fumble," and "turn over." It's no surprise that these things happen when you focus on them.

Instead, focus on the things you do want to happen. Tell yourself, "Watch the seams of the ball," "Make contact," "Tuck the ball in tightly," and "Get a good snap on this pass." Tell your mind and your body exactly what you want to have happen and let them go to work on making it happen.

VISUALIZATION performance area #9

As an athlete it is important to develop your skills to the point where they become automatic, especially under pressure. Although nothing can replace the endless hours of practice that are required to make physical skills automatic, you can enhance your ability to perform your sport skills automatically by using visualization.

Visualization or imagery is a proven tool of top-level athletes. Many successful athletes use imagery to create the perfect performance, to see and feel themselves perform at their highest potential. They also re-create past successful performances, calling to mind what they saw, felt, and thought. This kind of visualization allows athletes to create their performance twice: once in the mind and once when they actually perform the act they have visualized. In addition, visualization helps manage your emotions, build your confidence, refine your skills, improve focus at practice and prepare you for competition.

I like to think of visualization as mental movie making. Picture yourself sitting in a theater watching a favorite movie. What images do you see as you look at the screen? What colors do you see? Who are the main characters? Who are the actors playing these characters? What are they doing? Now imagine yourself watching a different movie, one in which you're the star. This movie will feature you performing at your absolute best at your sport. Imagine what you look like on the big screen. What are you wearing? How are you standing? What expression do you have on your face? Picture the opponent, the playing area, the fans, your coach, the referee. Make your images as vivid as possible. Engage all of your senses as you fill out the scene: sight, sound, touch, smell, and taste. Watch yourself as you perform at your highest potential. Bring up all the emotional pieces as well: how it feels to perform well, to connect with your teammates, and so on.

In order to realize your potential as an athlete, make this movie again and again in your mind until it is vivid and believable. This technique actually enhances learning. During visualization, you mentally become the performer and practice the skills in your mind. We learn new skills faster using a combination of physical practice and mental imagery than using either one alone. The technique is so powerful that the reverse is also true: negative imagery can actually hurt performance.

In addition, you can change your emotional state by evoking the appropriate images during visualization. The chemistry of billions of cells within your body changes in response to what you imagine. In other words, you can change your emotional state by evoking the appropriate images during visualization.

In short, you can use visualization to improve your physical, mental, and emotional skills. Here are a few things athletes often visualize:

Technical and tactical skills: When you are learning a new skill or changing a technique, watch someone perform the task correctly and then mentally place yourself in that role. Become the performer and practice the skill in your mind. Break the skill down into its key parts and pay attention to how one part transitions into the next. Gradually build your sessions to the point where the transitions are seamless. Enhance your mental rehearsal with "kinesthetic rehearsal" by adding movement to the exercise. Use the actual muscle groups involved in the skill and be as active as you can in the situation. There is no limit to the amount of time you should spend on rehearsing skills. The beauty of mental rehearsal is that there's no wear and tear on your body.

Best performances: Go back in your mind and select one of your best performances. Remember everything about it. What did you do to prepare? What you were wearing? Where were you? What was the weather like? Who were you competing against? Who was watching? Remember all the things you saw and heard during the competition, your thoughts and feelings, what you did between plays, how you handled mistakes, how you handled success, and how the competition ended.

Breakthroughs: Visualize overcoming an obstacle you face in your sport. Examples include certain competitors, specific plays or skills, weather conditions, rounds in a tournament, tiebreakers, and overtime.

Big competitions: Visualize the big match, game, or meet in your mind before you ever set foot on the playing surface. See, hear, and feel it go exactly the way you would like it to go. Like an actor going through dress rehearsal, practice your responses to challenges and situations that might occur. Think about what you will say, how you will act, and what you will think.

Achieving long-term goals: See yourself accomplishing the long-term vision you have set for yourself. Imagine how you will feel when you achieve your goal. Think of the excitement and satisfaction. Visualize the reactions, of family, coaches, and teammates. Feel the way your body will feel. Make the day come alive.

Visualization is a skill you can practice almost any time and any-place. To develop your visualization skills, start by using non-threatening, non-stressful images. From there, progress to visualizing sport skills

and finally competitive situations. Keep in mind that visualization is most effective when your mind is calm and your body is relaxed. Just like physical skills, it can be improved only through practice. Spend at least ten to fifteen minutes each day working on visualization.

Using music during visualization training can reinforce the physiological mechanism you are working to elicit. In their book, *The Music Effect: Music Physiology and Clinical Applications,* Daniel J. Schneck and Dorita S. Berger write, "Music is well known to have a significant effect on physiology and is widely used as an effective therapeutic tool in stress and pain management, rehabilitation, and behavior modification" (Schneck and Berger 2006, p. 54). Different music will bring about different emotions: instrumentals and new age music tend to be more calming, whereas rock pumps people up. Experiment until you find what works for you.

Daily Life

In addition to the physical, emotional, and mental elements of competition, there is another important aspect we can't overlook: how athletes handle their daily lives. When I coached tennis at the Division I level, I saw that we had our physical, emotional, and mental training in order, yet we still managed to under-perform. The inescapable question was, what's missing?

What I came to recognize was that athletes need to maintain their personal integrity and to manage their daily commitments. You have important commitments to time management, relationships, academics or work, and so on. When these commitments are broken, they drain energy from you and distract your focus and purpose. A complete training program needs to recognize that how you manage your daily life and commitments has a decided impact on how well you play your game.

TIME MANAGEMENT area #10

Each of us has our to-do lists, and we are supposed to be proficient at "time management" in order to get everything done. For student athletes, the time-management challenge involves a balancing act between school, sports, homework, social time, personal time, and family activities. Athletes who are no longer in school face a similarly daunting challenge.

There are literally thousands of books that claim to teach us how to juggle all of these tasks and effectively manage our time. Of course, "time management" is a bit of a misnomer. No one can literally manage time—time just keeps moving regardless of what we do. However, what we choose to *do* with our precious time determines the degree to which we will fulfill our potential and realize our dreams.

Accomplishing your dreams does not happen by accident; it is the result of planning. You have the same amount of time as your competitors do. How you *choose* to spend that time is what matters most. Do your choices support your quest for success? Do they move you closer to your dream? Chances are that your choices won't enhance your success unless you do some thoughtful planning. Planning your activities allows you to focus on the things that you decide matter the most.

Effective planning is a skill, not a gift. Like all skills, it can be developed with practice. The key is self-discipline, which is the path to self-reliance. In the heat of battle, you must rely on yourself. You alone hit, shoot, kick, or catch the ball; you alone run each step or swim each stroke. It's in your use of time that you will develop the self-discipline necessary to become self-reliant.

Successful athletes don't just do things differently. They do different things!

Successful athletes are proactive in their lives—they plan, perform, evaluate, and plan some more. Above all, they organize and manage their time around what's important to them based on their values and beliefs. They put their time and attention on the things in their lives that produce results. The following popular story illustrates my point.

A professor stood before his class with some items on the desk. When the final student was seated, the professor picked up a large glass jar and proceeded to fill it with rocks about two inches in diameter.

The professor asked the students whether the jar was full. They agreed that it was.

He then picked up a box of pebbles and added them to the jar, shaking it lightly. The pebbles rolled into the open areas between the rocks.

"Is the jar filled now?" the professor asked. "Yes," said the students.

The professor picked up a bag of sand and poured it into the jar. The sand settled in the spaces between the rocks and pebbles.

Once more the professor asked whether the jar was full. After some thinking the students said that it was.

The professor then took a large glass of water and poured all of it into the jar.

After the laughter subsided, the professor spoke.

"I want you to recognize that this jar represents your life," he said. "The rocks are the important things in your life: your family, your friends, your health things that if everything else was lost and only they remained, your life would still be full.

"The pebbles are the other things that matter, like school, your sport or job, and your car.

"The sand is everything else. The small stuff.

"If fill the jar with sand first, there is no room for the pebbles or the rocks. The same goes for your life. If you spend all your time and energy on the small stuff, you will never have room for the things that are important to you.

"Pay attention to the things that are critical to your happiness and success. Take care of the rocks first the things that really matter. Set your priorities. The rest is just sand."

Make a commitment to better time management. This includes setting aside time (!) for weekly and daily planning. I noticed during my years at Cal that the most successful student-athletes used some sort of tool to manage their activities. The tools ran the gamut from small, free calendars obtained from the bookstore to elaborate day timers or sophisticated electronic organizers. The choice of tool was personal, but the results were the same. Pick your own tool, and take twenty-five to thirty minutes at the beginning of each week to plan the week ahead. Sit down in a quiet place, take out your calendar or day planner, and decide what you want to accomplish during the coming week. Remember to filter out the unimportant things. Reconnect with your vision, your dream. Review your goals and set objectives for the week.

 ▶ Plan to complete assignments one or two days before they are actually due just in case something unexpected comes up.

Follow up by spending ten to fifteen minutes each day reviewing and revising your plan. Ask yourself, "What can I do today that will move me closer to realizing my vision?" Base your day's actions on your answer.

ACADEMICS performance area **#11**

"How you do anything is how you do everything" is one of my favorite Cheri Huber quotes. If you're a student athlete, taking care of business in the classroom pays dividends on the playing field. If you care about your performance in the classroom and you're not doing so well there, that stress will take a toll on your athletic performance. Even if you care little about your performance in school, the stress created by badgering parents and teachers, as well as potential eligibility questions, will impede your ability to perform at your best.

It's important, then, to manage your schoolwork. Use your planning skills to make sure you don't fall behind. At the beginning of each term, transfer the due dates for assignments, papers, and projects, as well as exam dates, to your planner. Break the assignments, papers, and projects into smaller steps. Then work backwards and create mini due dates for each step along the way. When you plan each week, transfer the mini due dates from your planner to your weekly calendar.

FUN performance area **#12**

We can get so consumed with our sport that we forget to have fun. Even before we reach high school, many of us are taught to repress fun as we go about the serious business of school. Yet the physiology of fun is a close profile to the athletic "zone." Laughter, humor, and play are powerful forms of recovery. They enable you to move almost effortlessly from negativity into a positive energy state.

Laughter is a natural breathing technique, and it has a cleansing and revitalizing effect as well. It originates in the solar plexus, the seat of bodily energy. Laughter alternatively relaxes and tightens your muscles and leaves them in a state of relaxation. It releases endorphins, which cause euphoria and reduce pain. Increasing evidence suggest that laughter is good medicine for both the body and the mind.

training tip ▶ Spend time with people who make you laugh. Watch funny videos. Collect and share jokes or other humorous material. Listen to comedians on your Mp3 player.

RELATIONSHIPS performance area #13

The people you surround yourself with directly influence your performance. No elite athlete—in fact, no successful person—rises to the top alone. It takes a strong supporting cast: parents, coaches, trainers, siblings, teachers, and friends. They keep you grounded and provide valuable support along your athletic journey.

It is up to you to build and maintain your support system. Failure to create and nurture effective relationships throughout your training environment will inevitably lead to a loss of motivation, burnout, illness, and even injury.

Top athletes create and support a culture of high performance through strong relationships. They support the people, teammates, coaches, teachers, family, and friends who support them. Ultimately, it serves your self-interest to maximize the energy, health, and well-being of all the individuals who surround you.

> Look for ways to support the people who support you. Make time for those closest to you in your life. Eat a meal together, go to a movie, study together, and spend time together during holiday breaks. ◄ **training tip**

Take an active approach to nurturing relationships that are rewarding for both parties. Look at Chart 7 on the next page. Imagine that your relationships are like bank accounts. In your relationships, do you make more deposits or withdrawals? What would be the balance of each account? Are any of them overdrawn?

Deposits	Withdrawals
+ Spending time together	− Gossiping
+ Sharing experiences	− Complaining
+ Talking	− Rolling your eyes
+ Really listening	− Criticizing
+ Making eye contact	− Laughing at them
+ Having fun together	− Ignoring or avoiding them
+ Supporting them	− Shaking your head
+ Giving pats on the back	− Fighting
+ Laughing with them	− Blowing them off
+ Smiling	− Being judgemental

CHART 7. ASSESSING RELATIONSHIP ACCOUNTS

ENVIRONMENT performance area #14

High-performance athletes take responsibility for their immediate environment and its influence on them.
They structure their environment in ways to make it more "user friendly." They customize and care for the places that support them (home, dorm room, gym, training room, locker room); and they respect the things that they use along their journey (equipment, food, clothes).

Your Space

Does your space at home support your success? Can you find what you need in a few seconds? Or is your home space a disaster area? How about your locker? Is it a black hole where things mysteriously disappear? When you leave the locker room, can people tell you were there by the trail of trash? How about the training room? Where does your tape end up after you cut it off? How about your ice bag? How about your water or sport drink cup? Do you clean up after yourself, or do others have to pick up after you? Without attending to your environment, you create stress for yourself and potentially others. Pay attention!

Tools of Your Trade

Think about your equipment. Is it in good shape? Do you take care of it? Do you know where it is? What about your uniform? Your practice gear? Do you get your bag turned in on time? Do you know where your water bottle is right now?

Conclusion

This chapter has introduced the fourteen key performance areas in the Game Face Training Program. Together, they are the foundation of the Game Face Routine—the key to athletic success.

These fourteen areas are a reflection of my own journey as an athlete and a coach. I was always looking for an edge for myself and my players. In my studies, I progressed from exercise physiology to sports nutrition and finally a graduate degree in sport psychology. Along the way I discovered that the fourteen areas in the Game Face Training Program have a significant effect on Game Face and the quality of athletic performance.

So how do you keep track of all fourteen areas? And how do you turn the concepts you've learned so far into a customized Game Face Routine and Training Program? The next chapter presents some powerful tools.

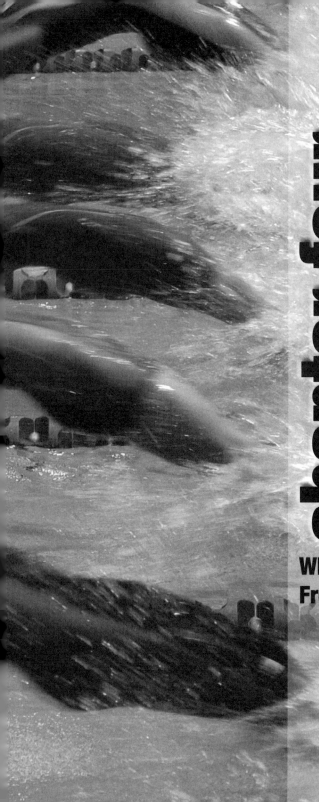

chapter four

Where to Go
From Here

Where to Go from Here

Now that you've been introduced to the Game Face system, it's time for you to create your own unique Game Face Routine and Game Face Training Program. You can find a number of resources to help you at www.CoachToon.com. However, with the content provided in this short book, you can go a long way toward designing and implementing your own personal Game Face system. This chapter gives you some suggestions for getting started.

Begin by Studying Role Models

A great place to start developing your Game Face system is to do exactly what Dr. Loehr did with elite tennis players and what I did at Cal: study top athletes in your sport. Success leaves traces, so study the best and imitate them.

Keep a few things in mind when you choose a role model to study. First, find athletes who are performing at a higher level than you, whether they compete at the high school, college, professional, or Olympic levels. Second, look for athletes whose temperament is similar to yours. If you are more of a fiery competitor, look for the Rafael Nadals, Abby Wambachs, or Kevin Garnetts of your sport. If you tend to be a calm, cool, and collected competitor, look for the Tim Duncans, Peyton Mannings, and Lorena Ochoas. Studying accomplished athletes who are similar to you in personality type is more important than selecting your favorite stars. Attempting to develop and use a Game Face Routine that goes against your emotional grain will be very un-comfortable and will not produce the results you are looking for. Third, make sure the athletes you choose to study consistently perform under pressure. Emulate the true role models in your sport, the ones who have achieved sustained success. Beyond their talent and skill, what separates consistently successful performers from ordinary athletes is their ability to bring their game to life when they need it most. Create a profile of each one, paying special attention to the Game Face factors you've learned about in this book.

How do you study these great athletes? It's ideal to see them perform live. Watching athletes in person at the college or high school level is relatively easy and affordable, so seek out opportuni-ties in your area. Keep in mind that an athlete doesn't have to be a well-known star to be worth studying and emulating. While professional or Olympic competi-tions may be difficult (and expen-sive) to get into, you might be able to observe some athletes at this level in person during practice sessions or exhibition events. Check out the teams and train-ing facilities in your area and see what's possible. For athletes at any level, see if you can take some video while you're observing. Explain what you are doing and that the footage is for personal use only. There's no harm in asking!

When you aren't able to watch top athletes in person, you'll have to rely on television. Unfortunately, TV coverage focuses primarily on the action and not on what's happening between plays, but you can pick up some valuable points if you are diligent and pay attention.

Your goal, of course, is to carefully study—and ideally make video recordings—of what your role models do between plays. Structure your observations around the 4 R's.

Reaction. Watch your role models' posture and demeanor immediately after a play. Note their reactions to different kinds of stimuli and events, such as

+ scoring
+ being scored upon
+ mistakes
+ fouls
+ contact
+ turnovers (theirs or a teammate's)
+ coaching
+ crowd noise

Recovery. Notice what the athletes do to recover energy and focus. Watch for their behavior in these situations:

+ between points, periods, plays, routines, or shots
+ during stoppages in play, time outs, penalties, and intermissions
+ sitting on the bench

Readiness. Observe the athletes as they near the re-start position for the next play. Notice such things as these:

+ where they stop just before the action resumes
+ their posture
+ where they are looking, what their visual focus is

Ritual. Watch what athletes do when they reach the re-start position. Observe their rituals in situations like these:

+ just before hitting, shooting, or kicking the ball
+ just before running, jumping, diving, or moving into action

Note how the athletes use elements of the 4 R's to maintain their composure during competition. Look for patterns and begin to describe their Game Face Routines in your own words. Write the routines down.

Then describe them to teammates, coaches, or friends and see if they agree. Try acting out some of your role models' routines as if you were playing a game of charades and see whether your teammates can guess who you are emulating. You might even make a video of yourself performing the routines, and then critique your performance.

Add Elements of Your Own to Your Game Face Routine

Imitating role models can get you started on creating a unique Game Face Routine. You also need to add your own elements to the mix as you find what *you* do between plays when you perform well.

Visualization can be a useful technique in this connection. Recall two or three of your best athletic performances to date. Spend time

visualizing each one in great detail. What were you thinking about? What were you saying to yourself? How were you behaving? Focus primarily on what the 4 R's looked like in each case. Pay attention to the same situations and behaviors that you studied when you observed your role models, but this time study yourself. Identify any behaviors that may have helped you achieve your best level of performance.

Now write down your 4 R's. Describe each one in detail. Next, compare your notes with the ones you wrote about your role models. Create a composite from the two sets of notes and come up with a concise, clear description of your 4 R's.

Continue to define your 4 R's by using them at practice. Put them to the test under relatively safe conditions. Look for as many ways to incorporate your routine into your training as possible. Use your routine between skill drills, during scrimmages, and even during conditioning. In the beginning, you want to use practice sessions to clarify each step. Eventually, using your Game Face Routine during practice will strengthen it and embed it into your being. The goal is to make it automatic under pressure.

Refine Your Game Face Routine

Once you've developed your personal Game Face Routine, continue to refine it as you incorporate it in competition. How does it hold up under true competitive pressure? Include each of the 4 R's in your post-competition evaluation. How did you do? What worked well? What didn't work so well? What was missing? Take notes, make adjustments, and work on those areas in practice.

Let's now take a look at what you can expect as you explore, develop, and refine your Game Face Routine. Here are a few common questions or concerns you may encounter along your Game Face journey:

How long does it take for my routine to become automatic so I don't have to think about it?

It's up to you. I have seen a few athletes incorporate their routine seamlessly into competition within two weeks of designing it. They got into it, studied the best in their sport, and immediately started applying pieces during practice. They set their minds to it and worked on it daily. On average, most of my students saw results within a month of designing and applying their routines.

Am I going to look like a dork doing this?

Remember, one person's dork is another person's ham. Chances are you may feel a bit self-conscious at first. If you're more on the reserved side, doing anything new and different may be uncomfortable. My students who have a hidden actor in them get into it, ham it up, and have fun with it. Remember, you will always have between-play time in your sport. You're doing something during this time, so why not do something to maximize it?

My coach is not into this stuff. What do I do?

Unfortunately, I hear this one far too often. Some coaches will resist. They are most comfortable focusing on the technical and tactical sides of their sport. If this your situation, you will have to work on your Game Face on your own. Enlist a teammate who can support you. It might be someone who seemingly has an instinctive routine. Ask your teammate to coach you on yours. Or you may find a teammate who is struggling in this area. Ask him or her to be your training partner. Give each other feedback on your progress.

I have also worked with many athletes whose coaches embrace this work. If you think your coach is receptive, set up a time to discuss your Game Face plans. Describe what you're up to, explain the 4 R's, and ask for support and feedback. Develop "trigger words" your coach can use to prompt desired behaviors in the moment. For trigger words to be effective, coach and athlete have to be on the same page regarding their meaning, so have the discussion off the playing field and come to an agreement about exactly what behavior the words are meant to trigger. Here's an example. When I worked with Amy Jensen on her Game Face Routine, she struggled with the first few seconds after a mistake or the loss of a point. We used the word *turn* to trigger the behavior of imme-

diately turning her back on the mistake. This was a crucial step for Amy in maintaining her Game Face, and the trigger reminded her to use her routine in the heat of the moment.

I'm afraid that if I don't follow my routine exactly, I'll lose.

Remember that your Game Face Routine is a tool, not a magic pill. It is one of many tools you will use during competition. Mastering your routine is not a guarantee for winning. Rather, your Game Face Routine is designed to help you perform at your best level.

Remember, too, that your routine is a work in progress. It takes time to define it and then refine it. I have yet to see an athlete use her or his Game Face Routine to perfection 100 percent

of the time during a competition, just as I have yet to see athletes execute their skills perfectly 100 percent of the time under pressure. Top athletes do the best they can in the moment and make minor adjustments along the way. What they *don't* do is blame their losses on anything outside of themselves and make massive changes to their techniques, tactics, or Game Face because of one loss.

This works great when I'm playing well. It's hard to do when I'm struggling.

You've got it. In many ways Game Face is what we naturally tend to do when things are going well. Yet it's one of the first things to go out the window when things are not going so well. The idea is to base your Game Face Routine on the things you do when you're performing at your best and to stick to them no matter what. If you're not performing as well as you'd like, be even more diligent about your routine to will help keep you in the game.

I already have so much to think about when I'm competing—how can I add even more?

You're right, you don't want one more thing to think about. That's why you create and define your Game Face Routine during practice and rehearse it until it becomes automatic. The more time, effort, and thought you put into training your Game Face routine during practice, the less you will have to focus on it during competition.

Implement a Customized Game Face Training Program

Once you have your Game Face Routine in place, it's time to support it with a customized Game Face Training Program. All the good work you put into developing and strengthening your Game Face Routine will be for naught if you don't attend to the fourteen key areas discussed in Chapter 3.

To help you keep track of how you're doing, I've developed a Game Face Training Log to use in rating your performance in the fourteen training areas each day (see Figure 10). At www.CoachToon.com you can download a sample log to use on your own computer.

Here's how you use the Game Face Training Log. In the Theme section at the top of the log, record a quality you want to bring to your training and performances in the coming week, such as confidence, toughness, intensity, focus, leadership, or energy. Next, write down specific actions you will take to achieve your goals in the Daily Actions section at the bottom of the log. An example might be, "Hit fifty extra serves before practice." Then, at the conclusion of each day, give yourself a grade (A through F) for each training area. You are the judge of what grades to give. The idea is not that you will earn all A's every day—that won't happen. Instead, you are looking for balance, consistency, and improvement. Being honest with your grades will help you identify strengths and weaknesses. Then you'll know what to work on and what to celebrate.

GAME FACE TRAINING LOG

Use the log during your competitive season. It isn't meant to be used year round. It can become monotonous and lose effectiveness if over used.

Remember, top athletes train each day so they can put their Game Face on when they need it most. They attend to the details of life and find ways to master them so they have plenty of energy available for competition. You want to build your own personal training program that helps you perform consistently at your highest level. The Game Face Training Log will help you accomplish this goal.

Conclusion

You now have all you need to get started on realizing your highest potential as an athlete. If you are willing to commit to building your Game Face Routine and supporting it with your personalized Game Face Training program, you will be ready to take on the competition. Too often this work is often ignored by athletes and coaches. Don't let that happen to you. This stuff is the difference maker!

We have covered a lot of material in relatively few pages. If you'd like further assistance in creating your Game Face Routine and Training program, please visit **www.CoachToon.com** where you'll find additional materials to support you on your journey to excellence.

Postscript:
Hey, Coach, Get Your Game Face On!

I want to conclude this book with a brief word to my fellow coaches.

Coach, speaking from over twenty years of experience, I know that we expect our athletes to show up for both competition and practice with their Game Face on. We want them to maintain their Game Face on the playing field no matter what. Do we hold ourselves to the same standard? The great ones do.

I believe the saying "A team is a reflection of its coach." The best coaches lead by example, so if you want your athletes to have great Game Faces, you need one, too. That means that all of the material covered in this book applies to you as well.

What does your Game Face Routine look like on the sidelines?

Think about the 4 R's and apply them to yourself in the midst of competition. How do you:

+ react to things that happen on the playing field?
+ recover between plays and during time outs, penalties, and intermissions?
+ get ready mentally for the action to resume?
+ use rituals to stay focused during the action?

I learned about my coaching Game Face the hard way. I was the assistant coach at the University of San Diego while working on my master's degree in sport psychology at San Diego State. For one of my course assignments I wore a portable microphone and was recorded on video while I coached a college tennis match. There were no action shots or cutaways, just me the entire time. In those days, college tennis matches averaged several hours. After thirty or forty minutes I forgot about the camera. Everything I did and said was recorded—*everything.* Then all the data—my words, body language, demeanor, and so on were sorted into various coaching and teaching effectiveness categories. Finally, I had the dubious pleasure of sitting down with my peers to watch the recording, review the data, and receive feedback. Talk about intense! I learned more about myself and my Game Face that day than from anything else I've ever done.

So, if you really want to know what your Game Face looks like, have someone record you during a competition—the bigger the competition, the better. Then summon up your courage and watch the recording. Really study yourself. See what your athletes see when they look toward the sideline during competition. Do they see Game Face, or do they see upset, frustration, and negativity? You set the tone for your players. Be sure to reflect back to them what you want to see on the playing field.

In this book I've stressed that athletes need to train their Game Face every day if they want to call upon it over the course of a tournament, a season, or a career. The same principle applies to us as coaches. If we want our athletes to attend to the details of life in order to be ready to compete, we need to do the same thing. For better or worse, our athletes watch our every move. Why not maximize this phenomenon and teach by example? Build your own personal training program, one that helps you consistently coach at your highest level. Using the Game Face Training Log will help you accomplish this goal.

Coach, if you would like more information on coaching Game Face in your sport, please visit my website at **www.CoachToon.com.** The site offers sport specific tips, tools and exercises to assist you in coaching Game Face with your athletes.

About the Author

From 1990-2004, Kathy Toon was the Associate Head Coach for Women's Tennis at the University of California-Berkeley, where she guided three doubles teams to NCAA championship victories. Her collegiate tennis coaching career includes earlier stops at the University of San Diego and Pepperdine University. Over a 23-year coaching career, Coach Toon has witnessed first hand the correlation between the behavior of competing athletes during "down time" and their ultimate athletic success.

Toon currently serves as a sports psychology and performance consultant to university and high school teams in the Bay Area. Her client list includes the University of California at Berkeley, where she works with the men's soccer, women's basketball, field hockey, golf and lacrosse teams. Other clients include Menlo High School, Marin Academy,

Campolindo High School, Katherine Delmar Burke School and the Riekes Center. In addition, organizations such as the ITA, USTA, LGPA, NCAA, Pac-10 and Prince Corporation have hired Coach Toon to lead performance seminars.

Coach Toon has served as a nationally-known trainer and product development manager for the nationally recognized Positive Coaching Alliance, has conducted hundreds of workshops for thousands of coaches, athletes and parents across the country. She authors a monthly column, "Through a Parents Eyes" in the PCA monthly newsletter. Toon is a frequent contributor to national publications such as *US Club Soccer, US Lacrosse Magazine, Ice Skating Institute EDGE* and *RES* and *AYSO Shorts.* You can reach her at www.CoachToon.com.

References

Loehr, James. 1994. *The new toughness training for sports: Mental, emotional, physical conditioning from one of the world's premier sports psychologists.* New York: Dutton.

Loehr, James. 1988. The 16 Second Cure. *World Tennis,* September: 80.

LPGA.com. 2006. www.LPGA.com.

Maas, James B. 1998. *Power sleep: The revolutionary program that prepares your mind for peak performance.* New York: Villard.

Mack, Gary, and David Casstevens. 2001. *Mind gym: An athlete's guide to inner excellence.* New York: Contemporary Books.

McDaniel, Pete. 2002. Tiger tips: how to drive it on target when the heat is on. *Golf Digest,* December: 34.

Schneck, Daniel J., and Dorita S. Berger. 2006. *The Music Effect: Music Physiology and Clinical Applications.* London and Philadelphia: Jessica Kingsley Publishers.

Photo Credits

The author would like to thank the following sources for allowing us to use the photographs listed by page number below.

California Media Relations (pages 2, 6, 11, 12, 15, 34, 46, 47, 68, 70, 80, 82, 83, 86, 89, 90, 93)

Teri Cluck (pages 20, 22, 23, 24, 25, 30, 38, 40, 44, 56, 57, 58, 61, 65, 72, 78, 82, 87, 93, 96)

Juan Kis (pages 9, 29, 97)

Stefanie Calkins (page 32)

Photography by Ruben (page 33)

Jessica Marshall (page 4)

James Poole (page 35, Sergio Garcia)

Sean Ware (page 35, Ben Gordon)

Gretchen Breuner (page 76)